Home-Made Made Hamster Toys

South Crater Ltd

www.southcrater.com

Contents

We Want to Hear from You

This book is published by South Crater Ltd, a small independent publisher of technical reference books. Proof reading and editing is managed in house.

We value your opinion and would like to hear your feedback. Feel free to get in touch to tell us what we are doing right, where corrections are needed or any topics you would like us to cover in future. Our email address is southcrater@virginmedia.com.

If you enjoy this publication, please leave a 5-star review on the online book store where you made your purchase.

We also welcome other approaches for collaboration on technical reference manuals or other training materials.

Ideas for a Second Volume

We especially welcome ideas for what to include in a second volume of Home-Made Hamster Toys. All contributors that submit and are accepted will be credited in writing and receive a free advance-copy of the book.

 # The Basics

Golden Rules

- Always use non-toxic glue
- Remove rough edges
- Coloured popsicle sticks must be non-toxic
- Avoid cedar and pine
- Hamsters must be supervised when there is any risk of harm

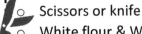

You Will Need

- Scissors or knife
- White flour & Water
- Glue/ glue gun
- Cardboard tubes (toilet roll inners)
- Popsicle sticks (birchwood)
- String (Jute/Hessian)
- Cardboard

Glue Choices

- Make your own glue by mixing white flour and water (1 part flour to 4 parts water). Make the mixture quite thin and then cook in a microwave to thicken.
- Buy a non-toxic glue such as Elmer's school glue or any white PVA glue
- Use non-toxic hot melt glue sticks in a hot glue gun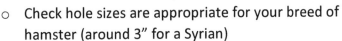

Remember

- Everything is likely to be chewed so always use hamster safe non-toxic products
- Check hole sizes are appropriate for your breed of hamster (around 3" for a Syrian)
- If in doubt seek the advice of a qualified small animal veterinarian

HAVE FUN

Techniques

Gluing

- Apply glue to one surface and wipe to a thinnish layer with a brush or your finger
- Only use as much as you need and remove excess with a damp cloth
- Press the second piece down and weight down or tape the pieces until the glue sets

Cutting

- When cutting with a craft knife use a cutting mat
- Hold the knife like a pencil
- For straight cuts use a metal ruler (not plastic)
- Apply just enough pressure and do not drag the knife through the material (leading to uneven cut)

Folding

- Working against the grain of corrugated cardboard produces a clean fold
- Mark and score the outside (viewable side) of your card
- Turn the cardboard over and fold using a ruler to keep a crisp line
- Use a creasing tool for a better fold

Coloring

- Use natural food colouring to dye your homemade hamster toys
- To make your own dye, chop colored food into small pieces and simmer in hot water. Allow to cool and strain through a sieve. Make sure not you use foods toxic to hamsters

Remember

It's Ok to be Wonky

All of the items shown in this manual can be made with little or no crafting experience. They will sometimes look just like the picture in the book and sometimes they might not.

It's OK – Wonky is fine. Your hamster will love a perfectly balanced seesaw that you have spent hours making no more than a wobbly, off-centre version that was knocked up in 20 minutes

The pictures of finished projects in this book were all made in super-quick time by a novice crafter. We are not afraid of our imperfections; you shouldn't be either.

Get Creative

Please feel free to add or remove items as you see fit for each project. Decorate (with Hamster friendly materials), decoupage and embellish to your heart's content … remembering that hammy might just eat it or pee on it in any case.

Safety first

None of these projects should have gaps where a hamster could get a limb trapped, have sharp edges or be positioned at a height where a fall injury could occur. If using melted hot glue, supervise your hamster to ensure it is not ingested in any quantity.

Treat Balls

What is it

These treat balls will make your hamster work for a treat
Great for enrichment and super simple to make

You Will Need

 Scissors

 Cardboard Tubes

 Hamster Treats

The Finished Product

9

Instructions

1 Take an empty cardboard tube and cut strips approx. 1cm wide. It doesn't matter if some are thicker than others.

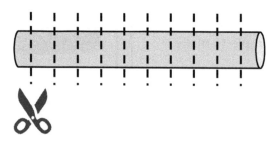

2 Arrange the cut rings of cardboard one inside another until they start to form a ball shape

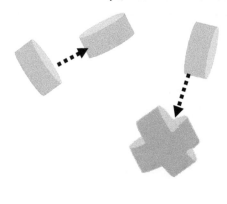

Keep adding rings until a ball shape is formed

3 Stuff your ball of cardboard rings with your hamsters' favourite treats

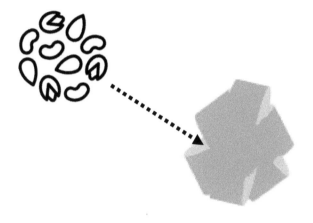

Project Complete

Notes

Cardboard Jump

What is it

A simple jump obstacle made from cardboard Simple to make from packaging offcuts. Use on its own or with the climbing wall and stick jumps for a complete obstacle course

You Will Need

 Corrugated Cardboard

 Scissors

 Glue

The Finished Product

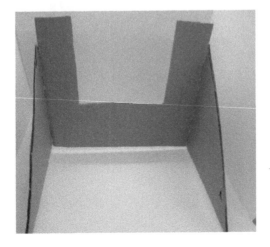

Instructions

1 Start by cutting two large triangles from corrugated cardboard. You can use old packaging as long as you have removed all packing tape or glue and the cardboard is not heavily printed.

2 Now cut out a rectangle and then make a cut out for the gap that your hamster will jump through

3 Assemble the jump by gluing the upright cut-out to the triangular supports.

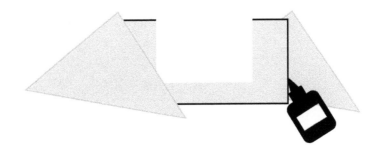

Project Complete

Notes
_____
_____
_____
_____
_____

Popsicle Stick Hurdles

What is it

A simple jump obstacle made from sticks
Use on its own or with the climbing wall and seesaw jumps for a complete obstacle course

You Will Need

 Popsicle Sticks

 Glue

The Finished Product

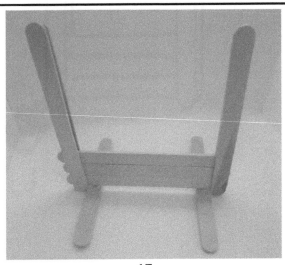

17

Instructions

1 create the body of the jump by gluing 3 or so sticks (depending on the height required) to an upright on either end

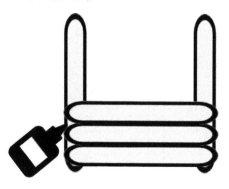

2 Complete the upright by gluing two more sticks vertically to sandwich the jump in the middle

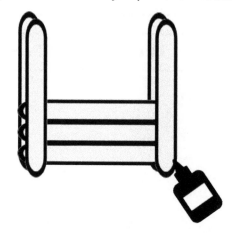

3 Glue two more sticks to the inside bottom corner of each side to make feet

Project Complete

Notes

_____

_____

_____

_____

_____

Shape Sorter Explorer

Level: Easy

What is it

An easy to make fun tube with different shaped holes for your hamster to explore

You Will Need

 Cardboard

 Scissors

 Glue

The Finished Product

Instructions

1 Cut a rectangular piece of cardboard that will be folded to make the tube and fold to make three sides with an overlap of approx. 1cm

Mark 3 folds

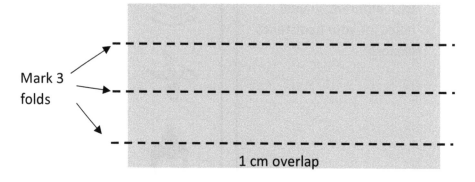

1 cm overlap

2 Cut a shaped hole of your choice (square, triangle, hexagonal etc) on the two sides, keeping within the creases

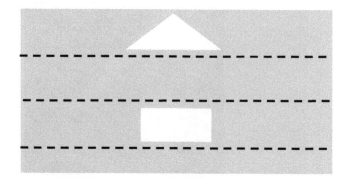

2 Fold along the crease lines and glue the 1cm flap to create a triangular tube

3 Drawing around the end of the tube as a template, cut two triangular end caps and cut a large diameter hole in each.

4 Carefully run a line of glue along each end of the triangular tube and attach an end cap.

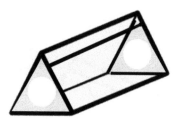

Project Complete

Notes

Hamster Fun House

What is it

A simple house for your hamster to explore, chill or just stash full of food

You Will Need

 Cardboard

 Scissors

 Glue

The Finished Product

Instructions

1 Start by constructing the sides of your hamster's house. Cut two rectangular pieces of card approximately 12 x 12 cm and then cut two small opening for windows.

2 Next make the two ends including the gable end. In one piece cut the opening for a door.

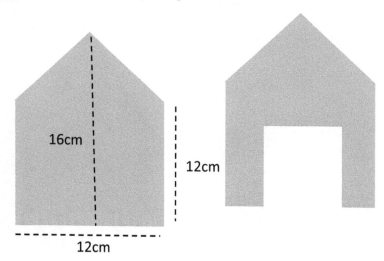

16cm

12cm

12cm

3 Glue the two ends to the sides to form the basic house shape.

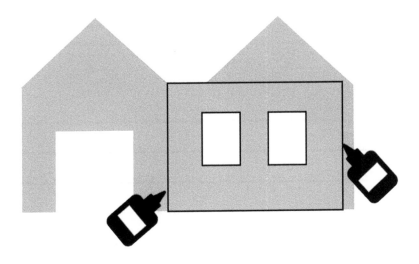

4 Cut two roof pieces approximately 12 x 16 cm and glue to the two gable ends overhanging the side walls.

Project Complete

Notes

_____

_____

_____

_____

_____

_____

Basic Ramp/Platform

What is it

This basic platform or ramp can be reused for many different applications like to make a seesaw, link different levels in the cage or to build a climbing wall

You Will Need

 Popsicle Sticks

 Glue

The Finished Product

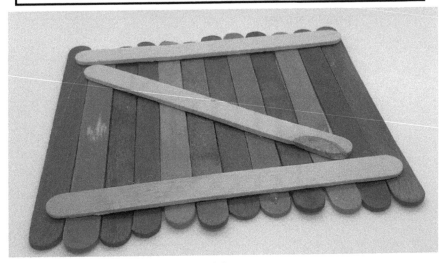

Instructions

1 Lay approx. 8- 12 popsicle sticks vertically side by side, ensuring that they are lined up top and bottom and touch each other leaving no gaps.

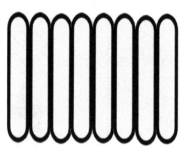

2 Glue 2 more popsicle sticks horizontally at the top and bottom of the stack, ensuring that that they overlap all of the existing sticks (adjusting the number of vertical sticks as required). Apply glue to the vertical sticks and press until set

3 Now glue a third stick to form a gate formation on the underside of the ramp. This additional stick gives the structure added stability

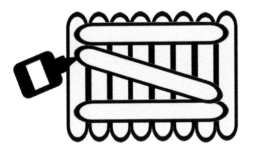

 You can trim the popsicle sticks with a craft knife if required to get a better fit. To make a longer ramp, join several platforms together by overlapping the horizontal sticks by 2 or 3 rows.

Project Complete

Notes

_____

_____

_____

_____

_____

_____

Climbing Wall

What is it

A climbing wall that can be used on its own or as part of a larger hamster obstacle course (see other items in this book)

You Will Need

 Popsicle Sticks

 Glue

The Finished Product

Instructions

1 Start by making the sides of an A-Frame by sandwiching 3 popsicle sticks at 90 – 100 degrees to form an A shape. Repeat so that you have 2 sides.

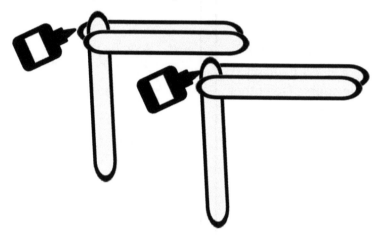

2 Construct 2 basic platforms (see page 24)

3 Glue the platforms to the A-frame with the flat sides facing out.

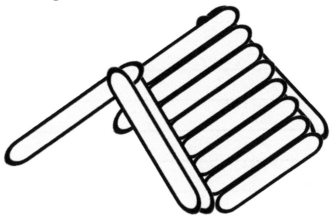

4 On each face of the climbing wall, glue 4 or 5 sticks equally distanced to help hammy grip as they climb. Use colored sticks to create contrast.

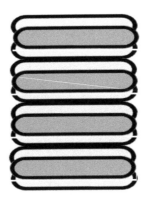

Project Complete

Notes

_____

_____

_____

_____

_____

_____

Teeter-Totter

What is it

A fun teeter-totter or see-saw that can be used with other projects to add to your hamsters obstacle course.

You Will Need

 Corrugated Cardboard

 Popsicle Sticks

 Glue

The Finished Product

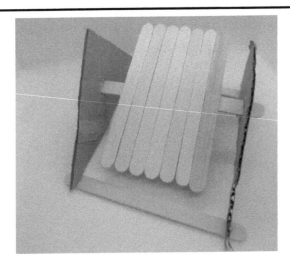

Instructions

1 Start by constructing a narrow platform and adding protruding sticks at the middle of the platform (these will act as the pivot for the see-saw and should stick out enough to ensure a good swinging action.

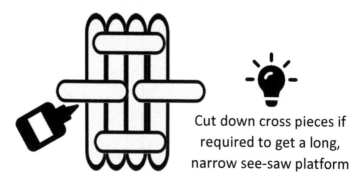

Cut down cross pieces if required to get a long, narrow see-saw platform

2 Cut two triangles from cardboard ensuring that the bottom edge is longer than the see-saw platform (for stability). Then carefully cut a semi-circular circle in the centre of each piece at least big enough for the popsicle stick to rotate inside.

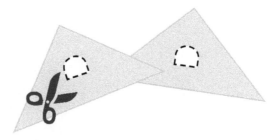

3 Glue the triangular uprights to 2 more sticks to make a firm base and finally thread the see-saw platform though the holes.

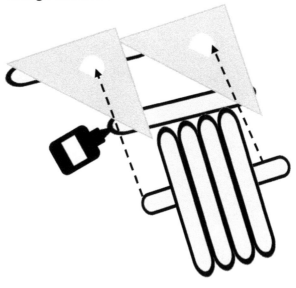

Project Complete

Notes

_____

_____

_____

_____

_____

_____

Hamster Hill

What is it

A stack of chewable, explorable cardboard tubes that also create the base for a super-fun climbing wall.

You Will Need

 Cardboard tubes

 Popsicle Sticks

 Glue

The Finished Product

41

Instructions

1 Start by gluing 5 cardboard tubes to form a stack with three on the base.

2 Construct 2 long basic platforms, long enough to cover the sides of the stack of tubes (see page 24) and on the flat side glue sticks at regular intervals to form a ladder.

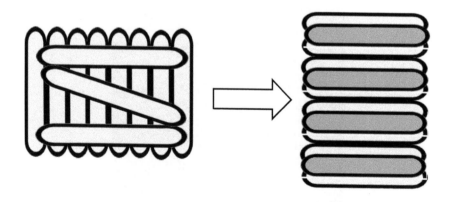

3 Glue the ladders to the side of the stack of cardboard tubes.

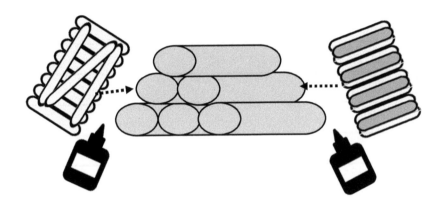

4 Make a flag by gluing a rectangle of paper to the top of a popsicle stick and glue to the back of the top most cardboard tube to claim this hill for all hamster-kind.

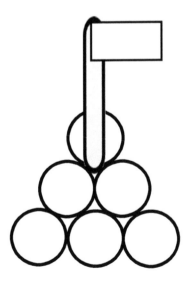

Project Complete

Notes

_____

_____

_____

_____

_____

_____

Aerial Tube Crawl

What is it

A mid-air suspended tube that hammy can crawl through, sit in or use as their favourite new food stash

You Will Need

 Cardboard tube

 Jute String

 Popsicle Sticks

 Glue

The Finished Product

Instructions

1 Start by making 3 square frames from 4 popsicle sticks each.

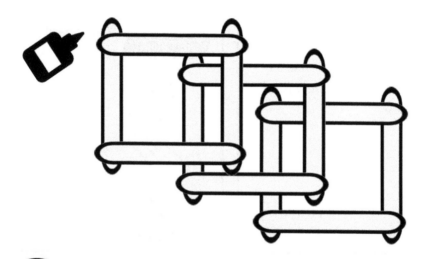

2 Attach 2 more popsicle sticks to the bottom of each frame to give them feet to stand on.

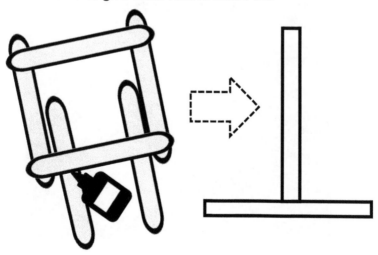

3 Cut a rectangle of carboard for a base and glue the three frames to the base.

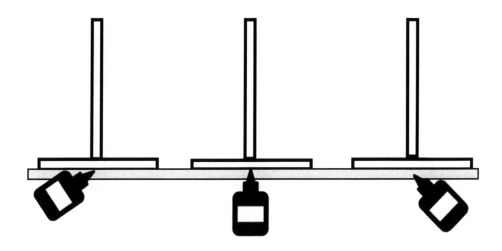

4 Thread a piece of just string through the centre of your cardboard tube and feed the tube though the centre of the frames. Tie at each end to suspend the tube.

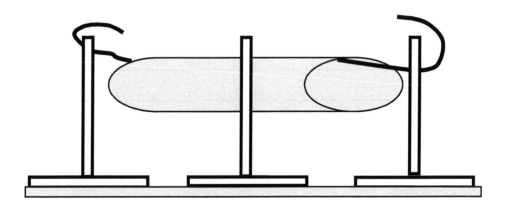

5 Cut a smaller rectangle from cardboard and glue across the top of the structure to make it more solid.

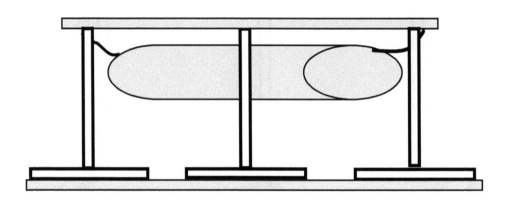

Project Complete
Notes

Swinging Platform

What is it

A swinging platform that will wiggle and jiggle as your hamster ties to climb aboard

You Will Need

 Jute String

 Popsicle Sticks

 Glue

The Finished Product

Instructions

1 To start, make a simple platform. A long, narrow one works best for this wobbly platform

2 Glue 3 popsicle sticks in an overlapping pattern to make a triangle. Repeat so that you have 2 upright supports

3 Connect the two upright triangles with two or 3 sticks to create a stable, freestanding platform.

4 Cut 2 equal lengths of jute string or sisal and glue to the bottom of the platform that you made earlier

5 Carefully tie the swinging platform to the A frame by passing the string over the top of the beam and securing with a knot (left-over-right then right-over

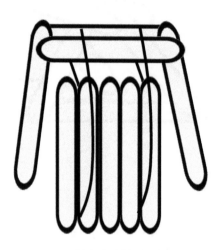

Project Complete

Notes

_____

_____

_____

_____

_____

_____

Rope Chew

What is it

A hanging decoration that your hamster will explore and probably chew

You Will Need

 Corrugated Cardboard

 Jute String

 Scissors

The Finished Product

Instructions

1 Cut between 4 and 6 different shapes from cardboard. You will need between 4 and 6 of each shape depending on the length of the chew rope you are making. Draw around cookie cutters if you need help drawing shapes

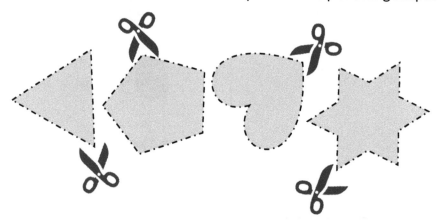

2 Using the sharp end of your scissors, or a sharp pencil make a hole in the centre of each shape. Placing the shape on a mound of modelling clay can help to do this safely.

3 Take a long piece of jute string, fold it into 3 to make an S-shape and tie a knot in one end and cut the other looped end to end up with 3 equal lengths

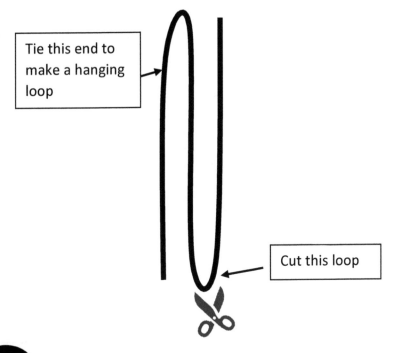

Tie this end to make a hanging loop

Cut this loop

4 Plait the three pieces too make a rope. For a simple plat take the right-hand string and bring it under the centre strand and over the left and keep repeating.

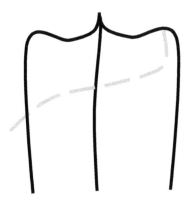

5 Thread one of each shape onto the platted rope and secure with a simple thumb knot. Repeat, varying the order of the shapes until you have all 4-6 groups threaded and finish with a thumb knot. Hang with the top loop.

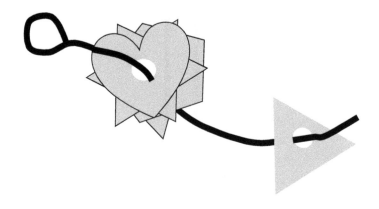

Project Complete

Notes

Amazing Maze

What is it

A fun maze for hamster to loose themselves in Make it more fun by stashing treats and filling different dead ends with bedding material to play in

You Will Need

 Cardboard

 Scissors

 Glue

The Finished Product

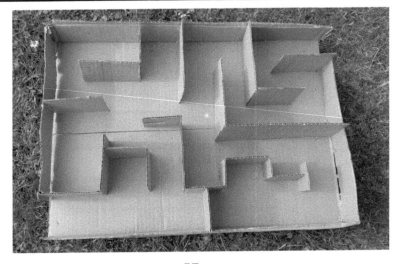

Instructions

1 Start by constructing a base on which to build your maze. We used an old box that we cut down to leave just the outside walls at 6cm tall.

2 Draw your maze shape on the inside of the base. Add a few dead ends and twists and turn to keep things interesting.

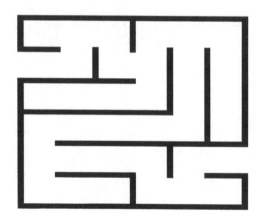

3 Cut carboard strips approximately 6cm high to the same length as the lines on your maze. Glue them along the lines and to each other for stability. Use masking tape to hold the pieces of wall in place whilst your glue dries (this one is easier with hot melt glue).

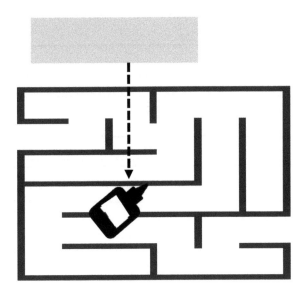

3 Remember to cut a hole in the wall for an entry to the maze and for an exit.

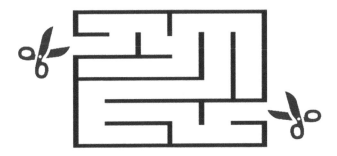

Project Complete

Notes

_____

_____

_____

_____

_____

_____

Picnic Table

What is it

A cute miniature picnic table your hamster can use as a climbing obstacle, a chew toy or who knows, maybe even as a table.

A little more tricky to build as its important to keep the table and seats square to the frame.

You Will Need

 Popsicle Sticks

 Glue

The Finished Product

61

Instructions

 Start by making the bench ends which are two simple A frames but it is important that the cross pieces are the same height on each end or the table and seats will not sit straight.

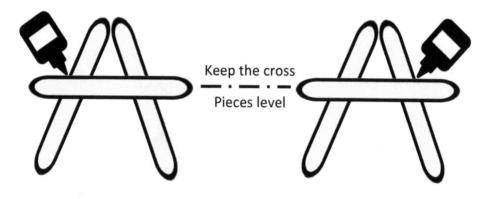

Keep the cross
Pieces level

2 Next construct a simple platform for the table top (see page 24)

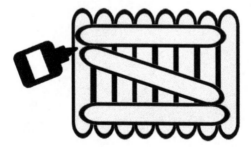

3 Make 2 more smaller platforms only 2 or 3 sticks wide for the seats

4 Glue the seats to the cross pieces on the A frame to make the bench.

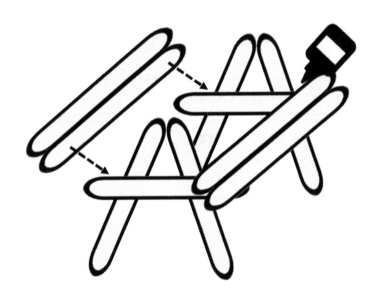

5 Complete the picnic bench by carefully gluing the table top across the top of the two A-frames.

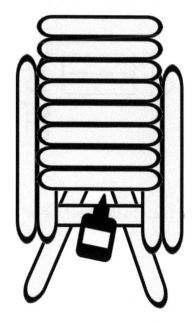

Project Complete

Notes

Rainbow Bridge

Level: Hard

What is it

A sweet little arched bridge that can be painted rainbow colors (using hamster safe vegetable-based paint colors)
A little tricky to make but worth the perseverance

You Will Need

 Cardboard

 Scissors

 Glue

The Finished Product

Instructions

1 Cut two arched shaped pieces from cardboard. We used a dinner plate as a template to get a nice curve on our arches.

22cm

X 2

2 Make the steps by cutting out two rectangles of cardboard approximately 3 x 6cm. Glue 2 pieces back-to-back to make one step. You will need between 5 and 7 steps (10 – 14 pieces in total) depending on spacing.

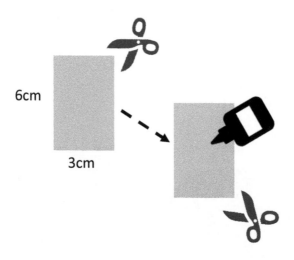

6cm

3cm

3 Space out the steps along your arch and mark the position of each one in pencil. Glue them in position on one side of the arch.

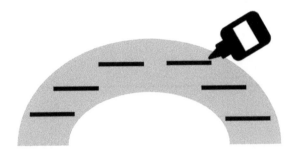

4 Now for the tricky part. Apply glue to the end of each step and carefully place the other side of the arched bridge on top, applying just enough pressure for the bridge to stick without it collapsing.

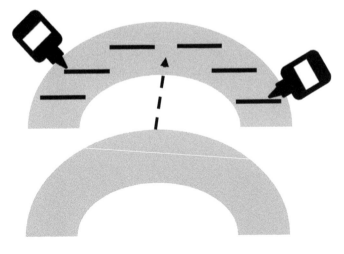

Project Complete

Notes

_____

_____

_____

_____

_____

_____

Other Publications

Complete Hamster Care

For All Popular Breeds

Full Color Inside

ISBN: 978-1-915634-01-6

Full Color Comprehensive hamster care manual for all popular breeds

Other Publications

Hamster Care Diary

ISBN: 979-8700735667

Amazon ASIN: B08VCL58BK

Track daily and weekly chores to make sure nothing gets forgotten.

Lightning Source UK Ltd.
Milton Keynes UK
UKHW020752200722
406119UK00009B/912